JESUS

LOVES

PROSTITUTES

By

Kay Christiane' Landwehr

Dedicated to my beloved late
husband

Jerald (Jerry) Landwehr

December 22 1936 – August 14, 2013

He was the kindest man I ever knew

FORWARD

If someone were to ask me for a picture of true unconditional love, I would tell them to look at Kay and her life. Kay exemplifies the love of God, always pursuing the hearts of those that have been neglected, lost, or forgotten. The love that she freely offers is not always freely received, but I've watched her persevere with courage through rejection, still offering forgiveness, kindness, and acceptance. When nobody, not even the girls, were willing to hear the message of unconditional love, she continued to knock on doors, bring gifts, and pray. Now, many are following in Kay's footsteps to carry God's love to the un-reached peoples in brothels and on street sides. Many girls have come to know God's love through Kay, not just by words, but through actions of true love and compassion. Not every miracle happens in an instant. Kay is a living example that sometimes it takes faithfulness over time; breaking up hard ground; choosing not to judge but to build relationship with the prostitutes, the pimps and the "tricks," until they see with their own eyes that God is love and He is in love with them. In the process, you show up, not with persuasive words, but the demonstration of power through love. You become the living epistle of God's free salvation and, like Kay, bring many to glory.

Sarah – Jane Vegas
Public Speaker & Social Justice Advocate

ACKNOWLEDGMENTS

Aglow International
Covenant Light House
Free International
Heritage Bible Church
International Church of Las Vegas
New Hope Fellowship
Spirit of Love
Trinity Assembly of God
Scott Leslie C.P.A.

Phillis Owen - for tatting the wonderful tatted flowers for the valentines

David and Maggie Dye – for providing phone for ministry

Norina Lyde - for her amazing photographic skills- (notice picture on back of book)

Kay Ermi – for crocheting the beautiful prayer shawls and bolas

Genie Walker – bookkeeper

Elaine Heath – providing anointing oil

Darcy & Don Schumacher – for opening their home to us for years

Timi Huskinson – an Octopus garden – provides flowers & plants

BOARD
Pastor Kay Landwehr – Founder and President
Pastors Al and Bev Weesner – Directors
Lupe Evangelisti – Secretary Treasurer

TEAM
Pastor Kay Landwehr
Lupe Evangelisti
Roseann Jones
Karen Cohen
Eddi Jean Collins
Sarah Jane Vegas
Kirsten Steele
Pastor Berta Johnson
Joanne Newman
Skye Bryant
Jane Histed – retired

There are many others who for years have baked cookies, Christmas breads, birthday cakes, cupcakes, made candy, donated candy, flowers and plants, and gathered beanie babies, stuffed animals – baskets and so many birthday gifts. To all who have donated your time, efforts and money to this ministry…

Please receive my heartfelt "Thank You!" God bless each and every one of you.

TABLE OF CONTENTS

INTRODUCTION

The purpose of this book, is to offer some truth about the legal brothels in the state of Nevada. The names of the working girls and the brothels where the girls worked have been changed. Some girls have asked to have their stories told in the "Interviews" section of this book and I have used their words as much as possible. Their stories are true.

My team and I have been visiting the legal brothels in this state for 10 years. We have made friends with many of the working girls, staff and owners in the brothels across the state. They know us as the "Church Ladies." Most look forward to our monthly visits.

When leaving, after visiting one of the brothels, one of the girls came running out to catch us before we drove away. "Kay, Kay, wait!!!" I went back and she came running to me. She shoved a donation into my hand. I started to refuse it but she said "You are the only church we have and we want to help out with the gas. Please, take it and don't forget us."

We do not disrupt or threaten in any way the girls

owners or clients. These brothels are legal in this state, and we respect their right to be in existence. Our intention is only to offer our gifts and unconditional love.

Just a word to those of you who would judge or criticize our friends in the brothels ... "DONT". However, if you are looking for someone to judge or criticize, I mean someone who is a real sinner, start by looking in the mirror.

"You may think you can condemn such people, but you are just as bad, and you have no excuse! When you say they are wicked and should be punished, you are condemning yourself, for you who judge others do these very same things." **Romans 2:1 (NLT)**

"The Spirit of the Lord God is upon Me, because the Lord has anointed me to preach good tidings to the poor; He has sent Me to heal the brokenhearted, to proclaim liberty to the captives, And the opening of the prison to those who are bound.

Isaiah 61:1(NKJ)

PANES OF PAIN

By Kay Christiane'

**Everything looks different…
Like looking through a windowpane…
that is dirty…
Or dripping with rain.**

**Looking through the dirty pane…
I see most everything that others do…
Except that some of the light is gone.
Looking through this pain…
Makes me feel depressed and hopeless.**

**Looking through the pane that is dripping with rain… Is most
difficult because of the extreme distortions…
Caused by the water streaming down the glass.**

**Looking through this pain…
Causes me to doubt my faith in my Creator…
And His love for me.**

**This Pit of pain is like being in an underground sewer
And looking up at the dirty rays of light
A man-hole would allow
To sift through the filthy air.**

<u>MY TESTIMONY</u>

First let me share with you a story about a little girl. Her mother tried for two years to have children. Finally to everyone's delight, she became pregnant. Her precious baby girl was born into a family that was anxiously awaiting her arrival.

The first child and grandchild. What a happy event. She was a beautiful baby. Her grandfather slept with her baby picture under his pillow. She made sentences at 18 months of age. Her parents were going to take her to Hollywood to become a child star, but her grandmother said no.

She was so cute and talented. When her parents had friends over to visit, she entertained them. She was the star, everyone loved her. Their own little Shirley Temple, making everyone laugh, quite the little actress, dancing and singing. Her Mom kept her hair in perfect ringlets all over her head. Her aunts made her beautiful clothes to wear. She was perfect and a good sweet little girl.

Suddenly when she was about three years old, she started having nightmares. No one could figure out what was wrong. Why was their little princess having these awful dreams?

The only memory I have been able to connect with is being in a dark basement with my Oregon grandfather – you know the one who slept with the little girl's baby picture under his pillow. I do remember feeling shame and that my body was very dirty. I can't remember what he did specifically, only that I was afraid of him. I would hide from him and I didn't want him to touch me. I did not want to sit on his lap. I didn't really hate him, but I didn't like him. I tried to avoid being around him.

He must have taken off my clothes because to this day

I have a fear of being without clothes on. I don't like looking at myself in the mirror without clothes on. It is a fear of being exposed.

I still do not have any memories of my early childhood. I was only able to write about the little girl, because so many stories were told about her at family gatherings by her mom and aunts and uncles.

When I was five my parents moved to Montana to be near my mother's parents. They had a big ranch with lots of wonderful animals. I loved my Montana grandparents and I have lots of wonderful memories of Montana. However, my Oregon experience set me up for yet another sexual molestation. I think I was in second grade when my mother's cousin raped me. Somehow my parents found out and I never saw him again.

I decided I didn't want to be a girl, and became a wild little tiny thing. Not wild as in promiscuous, but I would ride horses crazy fast, and became a tomboy. Not homosexual, just a wild child. I didn't like dresses and I didn't like boys. Later in high school I became a "tough girl." I beat up other girls.
It was then I was pursued by my Dad's boss. He hired me to clean his house. He had lots of money and was

willing to spend it on me. Again, raped. I was quiet, never told, but I became very controlling and demanding. He bought me expensive clothes and even paid for my first semester in college.

What a great actress I had become. In college I was voted "Spectator Girl," was featured in the program for the football team's games, Queen of the Peppermint Prince Ball, chosen to be an "Angel Flight," an honorary ROTC marching band, second lieutenant. Of course my major was in Voice and my minor was in Ballet.

I had to be in style, so I took flying lessons. Also it was important for me to learn how to smoke cigarettes. It took a couple of weeks. It made me so sick. I remember throwing up after smoking half a cigarette, but I kept trying until my poor body finally gave up and said, OK.

I didn't date much, no sex, became engaged to a very nice boy who really loved me. No sex. He joined the army and we were supposed to be married when he got out. I didn't really love him, so that never happened. I don't think I was capable of love at that point.

During the Christmas break I went on a skiing trip with

him. Crashed and burned, came home on crutches, with my ankle badly sprained. Going back to school, I couldn't get to classes on time on crutches… and ballet??? My adviser suggested I take a break and come back the next semester. I did. I was bored out of my mind.

My Dad sent me to beauty school in Spokane, Washington. I went on crutches. Soon the school wanted to sponsor me in the Miss America pageant. My ankle was better, so I said, "OK, let's go"! I ran and ended up in the top five. I lost to the girl who was dating my first husband. She, along with 80 other girls in Spokane. Maybe he was a challenge, probably! Then I became pregnant. I don't believe in abortion, so we got married. Bad, bad, mistake. I had morning sickness so badly I thought I was going to die.

I was a very beautiful girl and had a perfect figure, 36, 26, 36. When my tummy grew I was so proud of my baby, but his father was not. He wouldn't be seen in public with me when I was pregnant. So now more shame about my body. It was a good excuse for him to continue with his single life and he didn't miss a beat, was constantly out with his girlfriends.

So more shame and of course it was my fault. I was the guilty one, and since he was ashamed of me and my body, I became even more ashamed of my body. He was seeing other women throughout my pregnancy, so I was alone most of the time. He was in the army, so I had to go the Air Force Hospital for prenatal care and delivery. We were treated like animals.

I did go to a specialist who told me that because of my hip measurements I would require a C-section. The Army would not OK it, so I had my precious son in the Air Force Hospital. I was in labor for three days after my water broke. No one told me about water breaking, so I thought I had wet the bed when it broke in the labor room. I was so ashamed.

No one was there with me. My husband had been sent away to play ping pong for the Army. My Mom and

Dad were 165 miles away and could not come. They were poor. My Dad was drinking and out of work. My Mom was working her fingers to the bone in her beauty shop, supporting my two brothers and sister. I was pretty much on my own.

I can remember watching other women coming into the

labor room, having their husbands and families with them, loving and encouraging them. Babies born and leaving, day after day. I watched them come and have their babies and go. Every day the pain got worse. I was terrified. I wanted my baby to live, but I truly wanted to die.

The last day I started screaming and my lips and face turned black and blue from screaming. The nurses were so cruel and told me to be quiet, I was disturbing everyone. Finally an eye, ear, nose and throat specialist delivered my son. I know now that God had to have been there, because we both lived through it.

 I adored him. He was a big baby, but fussy. I'm sure the difficult labor was very hard on him. When I took him home, I was so scared I was going to hurt him, I stayed awake watching him to make sure he was still breathing.

In those days there was absolutely no direction or education. You had no idea what to expect or what was normal. His father was busy chasing women. I vowed I would never have another child. However, there wasn't much for birth control in those days, so I soon became pregnant with my second child. When the doctor told me I was pregnant again, I actually told him he was a liar. I was sick. I couldn't believe it. I was sure I would die.

The marriage was a joke, a bad dream come true, a real nightmare. Husband constantly dating other women, never home, and when he was, constantly wanting sex. I of course submitted to him because I felt it was my fault he was seeing other women. I was never enough for him. It never occurred to me that he might be the wounded one. It must be my fault, after all, I didn't have a perfect body anymore, and that was my fault too.

Of course this marriage didn't last. A little slap escalated into a harder hit and eventually being thrown across the room. After 13 years of physical, emotional, and sexual abuse I asked him to leave and filed for divorce. My Dad and Mom offered to help me raise my children, so I planned to move back to Montana. Soon after I moved back, they were in a head-on collision. My Dad was killed and my Mom was in intensive care.

I had been in the real estate business in California and was planning to go into it in Montana. However, first I was also planning to go to Alaska, leave my three children with my parents. and become a prostitute for two years. Then I could come back and open my own business. The pipeline was going in at the time and girls up there were making a lot of money.

Since I was unable to do that, my Dad was gone, my Mom not well, I decided to stay in Montana and go into real estate there. The local broker wanted me to work for her. I agreed and went to a real estate convention with her in Helena, where I met my next husband. He was very wealthy, single, and very taken with the new girl in town. I needed money to keep and raise my children. He had lots of money and a desire for a beautiful wife to accompany him all over the country. So I married him for his money.

I did not love him, but he was a good looking older man and I could keep my precious children. I was kind and respectful. I served him well. His motive was wrong and mine certainly was. I don't really see the difference between me and the prostitutes working in the legal brothels. I sold my body to one man. They sell theirs to many. I think they are more honest than I was. The marriage lasted five years. He, of course, was having an affair with another woman. I, of course, felt it was my fault. Again, I wasn't enough.

I hope you can see the thread of abuse that has been

woven through my life from the age of 3. It seems like once it starts, an invisible sign appears across your back and another one appears across your chest that says, "abuse me". The only people who can read the sign are the abusers. They are drawn to you like a magnet. They do abuse you and you expect them to. However, what Satan meant for evil, God turned for good.

I started on a long road of recovery. It's been difficult and hard. Healing is always hard. I've made many mistakes, but I've lived through them and learned from them, and only by the grace of God am I somewhat sane today. Like Joyce Meyers says, my victory cry is, "I'm still here." So you can see, God has prepared me to go into the dark places to take his love and light to these precious girls. He took the abuse I suffered as a child and adult and Jesus healed me with his great compassion and unconditional love. It is that compassion and love that he uses to heal others.

Maybe I see pieces of myself in them. Pieces that God has healed in me. Maybe that is what I have to offer them. The pieces that God has healed in me. Maybe that's why it is important for more healing to take place in me so I will have even more to offer them. They know, you know, the places that are healed and the ones that are not, because when you are transparent, it all shows. When I am transparent, the love of God can be displayed through me and it is that love that makes others around me whole.

I previously talked about the "wild child." I think there is a good kind of rebellion in me that God is using to combat "acceptable sin," such as judging others, gossip, criticizing others and putting down other people. I do get very passionately upset from time to time about these kinds of injustices. I do see the negative effects in suffering that sin brings. The Holy Scriptures tell me that I am to hate sin and I do.

I am in a position where I get to see the wages of sin. It is in my face and it motivates me to continue to go into "dark places." To go to bring the light of Christ into them. That is my job. That is every Christian's job. To bring His light and love into the darkness. Not everyone is called to visit His precious prostitutes in the brothels, but everyone is called to bring His light and love into the darkness somewhere. There is plenty of darkness to be found. I cannot bring his light without bringing His love. Light without the love is a false light. You bring the love first and the light follows.

Sometimes I cry when I see the dilemma these girls are in. "Jesus wept" is the shortest verse in scripture and perhaps for me, the most profound. I'm sure Jesus is weeping with me. He is my only hope and He is their only hope. My job is to love them unconditionally. To listen to them, not to preach at them. To demonstrate God's love for them.

Bringing gifts, celebrating their birthdays, Christmas gifts, Easter baskets, offering prayer for their concerns, supplying them with CD's, DVD's, books, etc., at no charge. I believe the most important thing we can give them is the consistency or faithfulness of going back month after month, year after year. They know we will be back.

Is it hard, is it a sacrifice? Of course it is. People ask how we get in. It is very simple. By the grace and will of God. "God opens the doors no man can close, and closes doors, no man can open."

THE CRYSTAL

By Kay Christiane'

The soft breeze played with the crystal… Slowly
turning it here and there…

Causing it to catch the morning sun…
Transmitting fountains of liquid rainbows
everywhere…

A crystal is born of fire…
Made from the earth…
Transformed by fire…
It becomes transparent…
It has nothing to hide…
It keeps no secrets…

It was created by THE FIRE to transmit what is…
Sometimes THE WIND moves it…
To reflect THE LIGHT…
And it dances with joy…
As it displays…
Its lovely rainbows…
Of promise and life.

MOVING TO PAHRUMP – START OF BROTHEL MINISTRY

My late husband and I moved to Pahrump to get away from the City life of Las Vegas. Las Vegas is not animal friendly. We had animals and needed a place away from the city. After moving here we discovered there were two brothels in the Pahrump area. I felt God calling me to go visit them and check them out.

One of them served food, so my husband and I and another couple went out to Sheri's Ranch and had dinner. One of the girls gave us a tour.

I felt impressed by the Lord to go back once a week to "eat and pray." Since my husband wasn't into visiting a brothel once a week, I started looking and praying for someone to accompany me. It wasn't long before I met another lady at a local prayer meeting, who was very happy to visit the local brothels with me. We felt we were only to go out once a week to "eat and pray", so that is what we did.

The scriptures tell us not to despise small beginnings. I never dreamed at the time, that one day we would be driving approximately 1500 miles a month, all over the state of Nevada. To visit countless girls in the brothels.

We started praying that the local communities in different parts of the state would catch our vision and become involved in this ministry. Sure enough, we were able to establish House of the Rising Sun North, in Elko. They would cover the brothels on interstate 80.

Jane headed that team and has done an awesome job for a season. Sadly, she had to retire, but leadership of that team had been solidly established by that community, and the baton was handed over to Pastor Berta, who is also doing a super great job.

It was our goal to establish another local team in the Carson City/Reno area, which would save us traveling approximately 700 miles per month and release our local team to better serve the brothels in the south end of the state. We believe this is in the process of becoming a reality.

We are so grateful to God for the many other wonderful ministries available with whom we may network.

The unity and friendships we have been able to enjoy is

beyond wonderful. Currently our plan is to make the long trip (1500+ miles) once every three to six months. Whatever the Lord wants; to share ideas, stories, what is working well, and what isn't. But mostly to encourage one another, pray together and stay connected, on the same page.

Esse (left) and Lupe on an Easter run.

HOW TO LOVE A PROSTITUTE

By Esse Johnson

Jesus loves prostitutes. Not the profession, but the women caught in it. Some of His great, great, great grandmothers went down in history as righteous, despite harlotry. Tamar "played the harlot" with Judah (see Gen. 38); and, yet, he called her *"more righteous than I."* Rahab was a non-Jewess and a career prostitute, but *"she was shown to be right with God by her actions"* (Jas 2:25NLT) Both are matriarchs in the Davidic line. Jesus esteemed prostitutes above the religious rule-keepers: *"Truly I say to you that the tax collectors and prostitutes will get into the kingdom of God before you"* (Mt. 21:31 NASB). The "you" doesn't just refer to Pharisees. It's anyone counting the sins of others, and thinking themselves superior. Prostitutes have held a tender place in the heart of our Lord.

A Ministry of Kindness

Las Vegas is chock full of Jesus freaks. I love that God has called us here. There are a number of ministers in this area dedicated to loving and, whenever possible, rescuing girls from the sex trade, and I am the least of them. To be clear: we don't go in to push girls out. We go into the dark places to be light and love, and trust God for the rest. *Hookers for Jesus, The Cupcake Girls, XXX Church, Free International, True I.D., House of the Rising Sun (HRS), Stand 4 Justice Movement, , Purple Wings*—I'd love to tell you about all of them when we have some time. With HRS, my friends and I frequent the strip clubs, brothels and porn shops nearby. Sometimes, we get to pray for girls, and owners and "Madams," too. We bring them cookies and gifts. We give them free Bibles, Joyce Meyer books, teaching CDs, teddy bears, flowers and handwritten cards. We pray and speak into their lives every chance we get, but we wait on the Lord for the open doors.

Truly, it breaks my heart to leave them there in the snare. One day, I was just flat angry. I cried out to God, "When!" When was He going to *set the captives free?* Why did I have to go and see the bondage? Glimpse the beauty of their destiny juxtaposed against the tyranny of a satanic detour? Why did I feel so powerless?

And the Lord said:

"Do you think lightly of the riches of His kindness and tolerance and patience, not knowing that the kindness of God leads you to repentance?" (Romans 2:4 NASB)

Woo!! Abba showed me that kindness, the kindness shining from Him through us, carries great power. It holds a promise. It's the promise of repentance. I stand on that promise.

We do occasionally have earth-shaking encounters. Our ministry leader, Kay Landwehr, has not only led many working girls to Jesus, but she once baptized six girls using the brothel swimming pool---bikinis, stilettos and all! She was welcomed back several times to provide Bible study, also inside the brothel. Thereafter, the girls continued worship, prayer and Bible study on their own…inside the brothel!

On one occasion, a girl was glaring at my best friend and ministry partner, Sarah-Jane, as if she'd seen a ghost. After a while, she told Sarah-Jane about a dream she'd had. There was a battle between good and evil men. She stood in between them, a gun in her hand. In the distance beyond the good men, there was a church. A young woman emerged from the church, veiled and dressed in white. She was praying as she approached. The young woman came to her. She took the gun from her. The young woman was Sarah-Jane. Telling the story, the presence of God came so strongly inside that brothel that girls who hadn't met Him cried out, "God is here! I can feel Him!" They wept together. They prayed. That girl left the business shortly thereafter. We haven't heard of her whereabouts in months. But we haven't stopped praying.

Stories from the Inside

Most of the ladies we encounter have been victims of

abuse. One girl was gang raped by her boyfriend and friends at 12 years old. They taped it and threatened to make it public if she dared run (this is a common tactic). Then, they prostituted her on the streets. A guy tried to help her escape. They murdered him in front of her. She's been rescued and taken to a healing home twice, and run back to her pimp twice. She is in love with him. She's 16 now. We're praying.

We have another friend in the business who was first trafficked by her mother. She was probably groomed as a teenager. Now, her husband is her pimp. She is the sweetest; always so friendly and so thankful to us. She seems confident that this is her call in life, her contribution to the family she loves so much.

One absolutely stunning woman (she reminds me of Angelina Jolie) projected such confidence. She assured us that she loves Jesus, and I'm sure she does; that her work is a service to men in need; that she is a good person; and that she was happy with her life. Months later, she confided that she can't sleep at night.

She got into the business because her boyfriend physically beat her, took explicit pictures of her, and threatened to go public with them unless she went "to work." If she leaves, there's no telling what he might do, or what could happen to her daughter.

Recently, a woman came to "Angelina's" brothel and paid $5k for three girls. Then, she beat them because her husband had been cheating there. No one stopped her. After all, she was a paying customer.

Lots of girls in legal brothels are actually trafficked. Their pimps sent them in with threats, with violence, and with false promises. On top of high fees just to be in the brothel, the pimps take most of their earnings. And while some brothel owners are "nice," others have various control tactics up to and including torture.

Hope!

There's so much more I could tell you. The wonderful news is that God is moving. New safe houses are opening. Ministries are having success rescuing and reintegrating girls. Laws are being changed. The State of Nevada is working with police, in cooperation with the faith community, and little people like us to stop treating prostitutes like outcasts, and start getting them treatment. We're all learning how to love a prostitute.

If I may make such a request, please pray. Agree with us for the daughters caught in the snare, and the "Johns," too. *Father, send Your light. Set the captives free. Change the culture. Let the truth be told. Teach our societies the reality of life as a prostitute.*

THE BROTHELS

We need to remember the brothels are a different world… a subculture. When you go into a courtroom that is a different world. When you go into a doctor's office, you enter a different world. When you go into a church that too, is a different world. In all these different worlds, evil exists; however, so does God, and God wants every world in existence to be touched by Him. That is where Christians should come in. Jesus did not avoid sin. In fact, He sought it out. I believe as much or even more sin can be found in the churches. It is just disguised and hidden therein. At least the brothels don't pretend to be anything they are not. Their reason for being is to provide sex for those who want sex for a price. This exchange provides a job for the working girls. For the owners, it is a business, a legal business in Nevada.

The county commissioners in each county in Nevada, determine if brothels will be allowed or not. The Mustang Ranch became the first legal brothel in the State of Nevada in 1971. Before that, there were lots of brothels, but they operated in a "gray" area. They were "tolerated" and "zoned," but not really "legal." The government imposed rules on them, but they were not "legal." They have always been regulated by the county commissioners, who are the local government agencies.

In 1937 a law was enacted to require weekly health checks of all prostitutes. However, mandatory testing did not begin until 1986. The girls are required to be tested weekly for STD's, and monthly for HIV and Syphilis. In 1988, condoms became mandatory for oral sex and intercourse. While other states outlawed "red light" districts, Nevada made a special section of the tax code for brothels in 1971. According to Nevada State Law, legal brothels can only exist in counties with a population of less than 400,000. Prostitution is not legal in Las Vegas or Reno.

In 1979, a State Law was written that prohibited the advertising of brothels in counties where prostitution is not legal. Some brothels even advertise large parking spaces for truckers making long drives. However, most brothels advertise on the internet and on CB's for the truckers.

Prostitutes must be 21 years of age, except in Storey and Lyon Counties, where 18 years of age is acceptable to the county commissioners.

Some brothels have set prices, but the girls are "independent" contractors. so the prices are usually negotiable. However, they usually charge by the minute or hour, or sometimes by the sex act.

Every brothel is different. In some brothels, the girls may refuse a customer. In others they are not allowed to refuse a customer. When the customer enters the brothel, the girls are required to "line up" and introduce themselves. The customer then chooses the girl he prefers, then the two decide on what sex act is to be done and the price that will be charged.

In some brothels, if a girl does not show up for the lineups, she is fined by the establishment. In some counties the girls cannot leave the grounds for however long a time they have contracted to stay. These are called "lockdown" counties.

The girls are required to split their earnings evenly with brothel owners. But if a customer takes a taxi or limo to the establishment, the driver gets 30%, and the girl gets 20%. Sex workers are considered independent contractors and don't receive unemployment, retirement or health care benefits. They must register with the county sheriff's office, and pay $125 for their "sheriff's card" to be renewed every three months. In some cases they are not allowed to have cars.

In 2006, Lyon County made $316,000 in brothel fees and $25,000 in working permits for prostitutes. Some counties make as much as 25% of their business fees from legal brothels. The fees range anywhere from $200 in Lander County to $100,000 in Storey County per year.

Like any other business, brothels and prostitutes pay local fees and federal income tax. But, they do not have to pay a Nevada State tax. In 2005, brothel owners lobbied TO PAY state taxes because they were afraid for the legitimacy of their businesses. However, their request was denied. "The Governor just thinks it is a local government issue and not part of his agenda", spokesman Greg Bortolin told MSNBC. "He thinks as well, that he would be affirming the industry if he came out in support of the Bill.

THE OWNERS

Each brothel has its own set of rules – dos and don'ts. Each one is different. The owners are different. Their rules and regulations must be followed, or they can impose fines on the girls or terminate them. Some of the owners require free sex with their girls, some don't. Some treat the girls with kindness and respect, some don't.

Our ministry goal in dealing with the owners is pretty simple. When we ring that buzzer and are invited in to visit their brothel, the staff, the girls, and sometimes their customers, we are to bring in respect, good will and gifts. We are there to demonstrate Christ's love to all present. We are not there to judge or criticize anyone.

Over the years, several of the owners have given us gas money, and most all encourage us to come back. We have never, nor will we ever, insult their customers. We have even had customers give us "gas money" once they find out what we are there for, and how far we travel every month.

We have prayer for this ministry twice a week, at which time we often pray for the owners. What do we pray for them? We pray blessings for them! Many blessings, just like we would pray for anyone else. We are not a threat to the owners or anyone else. We make friends and build relationships with them. We don't tell them how to run their legal businesses.

When Bobby Davis recently sold her brothel, Shady Lady, and moved out of the state, she gave our ministry her car. A very nice car, with very low mileage. She told me how much she and her late husband, Jim, appreciated our visits every month. She also was grateful for the love and respect we showed her girls, staff, and her and Jim. How she appreciated the wonderful gifts we always left for everyone! Bobby said she wanted us to have her car so we would be able to continue visiting the other brothels around the state.

Sometimes, if we arrive at a brothel and it is mealtime, we are invited to eat with them. Often we are offered a bottle of water or a soda. A few of the owners are rude, but do let us leave gifts for the girls.

There is a couple who will not let us visit. We are not sure why, but we continue to leave gifts and pray blessings for them. Some of the owners and managers do sincerely care about the well-being of the girls. Just recently, while visiting with a manager, we learned that this manager had gone to bat for her girls, and was able to get the wording changed on the girls' sheriff's cards, deleting the word "prostitute" to "self-employed" or "independent contractor", so the girls would not be labeled, "prostitute" by the sheriff's office nor would it go on their permanent records as such.

GIFT GIVING AND SERVICES OF LOVE

Sarah-Jane Vegas on an Easter run.

THE ROCK

It has been our custom to bring gift bags to the girls at Christmas. A lady friend of ours spends summers on the Oregon Coast. She loves to pick up interesting rocks to paint and then write special sayings on them to give away as gifts. She had prepared 40 of these special rocks for us to include in the Christmas gift bags for the girls. Before Christmas that year, we passed out over 100 gift bags, so only 40 of them contained the gift rocks. We had no idea which girl got the bags with the rocks in them. One of the rocks was in the shape of a heart and said, "Jesus loves you." Months later I got a call that one of the girls had passed away and her mother wanted me to do a Celebration of Life Service for her. Her mother had found the heart-shaped rock saying, "Jesus Loves You," in her room and realized that we had given it to her. I agreed to do the service.

The girls don't save very many things. They travel pretty light. The fact that she saved that heart-shaped rock with the message, Jesus Loves You, must have been something very special to her. Praise God for the Rock of our salvation.

FOOT DETOXES

There is something special about washing someone's feet. Jesus washed the feet of his disciples. It is very personal. I had an ionic foot detox machine. So we put it to good use. We wanted to wash their feet. It was set up in a private room of the brothel and we would spread out our gifts (Bibles, books, CD's, lotions, etc.) on the bed.

The detox takes about ½ hour to complete the cycle. One of us would do the detox and the other would pray for her silently for ½ hour. After completing the detox cycle, we would get a fresh pan of warm water and wash her feet. Then her feet would be dried and anointed with anointing oil. After that she was invited to the gift area to select any of the displayed books, CD's, DVD's etc. that she wished to take. We never charge for anything.

The towels we used to dry her feet were donated by a special lady who purchased them and embroidered on them, "I am God's Girl." Each girl was given her towel to keep. It seems like once their feet were immersed in water for the detox, they would start sharing with us about their families and loved ones; sharing almost always about what their dreams and aspirations are.

I have never heard one share how she wanted to be a better prostitute. Most of them look at their current profession as temporary. Oftentimes they want to start a business, go back to finish school, or go on to further their education. We hear as many different dreams as there are girls.

These girls are real live human beings. They have dreams of a better life for themselves and their children, just like most of us. They are someone's daughter, granddaughter, mother, sister, wife, or friend. God created these women and the Holy Scriptures tell us that God loves His creation and he commands us to respect His creation.

Sarah-Jane showing a beautiful gift in van in front of a brothel.

The girls love inspirational books, especially Joyce Meyer.

Making and delivering Easter gifts. Lupe and Kay. Karen making cookie hearts with the team.

Our girls love their Beanie Babies!

Volunteers!

They are so good to us!

Flat tire in the desert. It took a trucker and a highway patrolman to save us. Praise Jesus! Things don't always go as planned, but God's plans are always right and true.

Esse, Kay, Eddie, and a packed Van at Thanksgiving.

THE WEDDING

Being an ordained pastor, I see my position as a pastor, with my church located on the inside of the brothels and my pews are bar stools. So far I have done three weddings and one Celebration of Life. The first wedding was a biker wedding. Two sisters wanted to marry two bikers. A double wedding. One of the sisters was a hostess in one of the brothels and heard I was a pastor. She and her fiancé contacted me and made arrangements to do a unique wedding. They wrote their vows which I added to the traditional vows. The wedding was held in a very nice park out in the desert. The reception was held inside the bar. The cake was exceptionally beautiful. Several motor cycle clubs had been invited. Immediately after they said, 'I do', the girls were whisked away on their new husband's motorcycles, long white wedding dresses and all.

Roseann Jones with homemade Christmas breads.

CHRISTMAS AT ANGELS LADIES

We were going further north on highway 95 and eventually made it into a day trip. Going north as far as Mina and returning back down 95. We drove to Mina in the morning, arriving around noon, then visited one of the brothels and the rest of the ranches on the way back.

We always try to make friends with everyone we encounter in the brothels, including the owner's staff and clients; whoever we meet, when we go in. I think it is important to remember that these brothels are legal in this state. It is always appropriate to respect others. It is not our job to judge or criticize them. We are to love others unconditionally.

The owner of Angels Ladies invited us to their Christmas dinner and we accepted. Christmas morning, Jerry and I traveled to Beatty to celebrate Christmas with the owners and their four girls and the girls' boyfriends (pimps). It was a wonderful celebration. One of the owners played his guitar and we sang Christmas carols and other old songs.

I pitched in and helped with getting the dinner ready. Then we all sat down to a beautiful turkey dinner. Mac, the owner, asked me to say a blessing over the food, which I did. It was amazing. One of the owner's had Christmas gifts for everyone, including us. After dinner, we opened our gifts. Everyone got a beautiful warm throw blanket. We sang more songs after dinner and some went for a walk.

It was definitely a very blessed Christmas. God's peace permeated the entire place. Peace on earth was there in the hearts of everyone, even if only for one day. When God touches a gathering of His people as He did that day, no one goes away unchanged. Every person there was blessed in some way. It was truly an encounter with our Creator.

Since we were visiting once a week, our presence was accepted and the girls began to look forward to our visits. They would come over to our table to visit with us when they were not busy. They quickly learned we were not a threat. We were Christians and cared about them. We did not judge or criticize them in any way.

As we became friends with some of the girls, we started bringing them little gifts. When we could find out their birthdays, we would bring them a home-baked birthday cake with candles, a little birthday gift and a card. The card was always signed with, "God danced the day you were born." Many of them had not celebrated their birthdays for years. Some never had.

As we sang Happy Birthday to them, more often than not we would see tears streaming down their precious faces. They realized that we did care for them and were actually demonstrating our love and God's love for them in a tangible way. "My little children, let us not love in word or in tongue, but in deed and in truth." (1John 3:18-NKJ)

CHURCH SERVICES AT SHERI'S RANCH

After we had been visiting for a couple of years, some of the girls wanted us to come on Sunday morning and offer church services for them. Nye County is a "lock-down" county, which means that once a girl had arrived and had her blood test done, she could not leave until she had completed her contract time. They could not be released to attend a local church service.

The brothel gave their permission and we started services in a separate little building on the property. Saturday I was busy making whole wheat honey muffins and putting butter and honey and assorted goodies in a picnic basket to take out to them. I also took my Karaoke machine and Christian CD's (mostly Michael W. Smith's CD, Stand) for a time of praise and worship. Of course we always had a supply of Joyce Meyer's resources on hand. (They all love Joyce).

Over they would come at 9 am Sunday morning in their furry slippers and heavy bathrobes. The building smelled like fresh brewed coffee and they dug into the muffins. The service began with a solid half hour of praise and worship music. Then I just talked to them about the love of Jesus and how much He loves them. Then I would close with offering them an opportunity to receive Him as their personal friend and savior. Every girl that came to these services were led to the Lord. We were allowed to go out six Sunday's in a row and then someone complained and we were no longer allowed to have services. However, we kept going out once a week to eat and pray, celebrate birthdays, and just be with the girls…

Six months later ---

Some of the girls told us they wanted to be baptized in water. There is a separate motel out there where the girls are not allowed which would give us access to the hot tub and pool. So we rented a room. We checked into the room, went over and ate dinner. About 9 pm we met six girls in bathing suits outside at the hot tub, ready to be baptized. Most of these girls had been saved at one of the six church services we had held six months previously. So we explained what water baptism was about and read scripture relating to it. The six girls were baptized in water. We also offered them communion. The girls wept at communion.

They were crying so hard that tissues wouldn't hold, so

they used their towels.

We retired to our room and listened to praise music the rest of the evening. One of the girls put on a Christian CD in the office that played out over the pool area. The girls told us later that it played day and night all weekend long.

THE STORM

By Kay Christiane'

Strong winds gathered gray clouds
together… Setting the stage for the
Storm.

Lightning struck like truth…
Shattering…cutting to the core…
Thunder followed…

Loudly shaking and dislodging…
Denial and half-truths…

Rain came…
Scrubbing and cleansing…

The SON burst forth…
Warming…
Healing…
Making whole.

THE LINEUP AT THE WILDCAT BROTHEL

Wildcat is a very small brothel. Tiny bar and tiny living room. Roseann is a very devout Christian. I have never heard her swear, or even come close to it. But she truly has a heart for the girls. She has been very active in this ministry from the beginning.

We had driven up to Wildcat to take our gifts into the girls and visit for a bit. The hostess warmly greeted us. We sat down at the bar and ordered our drinks. (Roseann's Coke and my water) I was busy talking to the bartender and Roseann was visiting with the two girls. A client came in unnoticed to both of us and asked for a lineup. So the two girls and Roseann stood in the lineup and when the girls introduced themselves to the client, "I'm Kitty, and I'm Missy." Roseann then said, "I'm Roseann." She did not realize she was in the lineup, nor did I. The client picked a girl, thank God, and Roseann came over to the bar, still not realizing she had been in the lineup. The hostess informed her she needed to go get her sheriff's card if she wanted to be in future lineups. Does God have a sense of humor or what!

VALENTINE COOKIES

One of the girls from Russia, a very tall and beautiful blond woman, shyly watched us from a distance. She wouldn't take much when we brought gifts, but stuck around and observed us.

For Valentine's Day that year we made sugar cookies in the shape of hearts and decorated them with pinks and reds. We stacked six cookies together in white netting and tied at the top with pink ribbon.

One of the local pastor's wives does tatting. Tatting is a lost art. I'm sure she learned it from her grandmother. This lovely lady tatted enough tiny flowers for us to be able to attach one tiny flower to the end of each ribbon.

The stacks of cookies were indeed a work of art. When we brought the cookies to the girls they were so blessed by them. They were so pretty. They hesitated to open the netting.

Our silent Russian observer came over to the table and picked up a cookie stack. She immediately noticed the tiny tatted flower. Suddenly she began talking to me about the tiny flower. I t seems that her grandmother had taught her to tat. Amazing what God will use to break the ice and melt their hearts. Happy Valentine's Day.

RAINDROPS OF LOVE

By Kay Christiane'

The rain…
Falling on the water…
Each drop…

Making an impact as it falls…
And is absorbed…
The Water…
Resisting the touch of the raindrops
Causing tiny splashes…

Your love is like the raindrops
Every tender touch…
Each loving look…
A precious raindrop.
Penetrating to the very core of me…
Invading my isolation
Splashing through the barrier of fear.
Each precious raindrop
Whispering I love you.
I love you. I love you.

Their love made me cry.

A SPECIAL WEDDING

They were so in love. You can always tell the way they looked at each other, and the tone of voice when they spoke to each other. They had been in love and living together for 26 years. They met at work and became very good friends. One day she said to him, "I don't want to live alone anymore." He then said to her, "I don't either." So they moved in together.

She was a hostess at one of the brothels we had been visiting for years. An avid reader, we gave her lots of reading material which she passed on to the "working girls." They had lots of problems with the government, as most everyone does these days. He was a lot older than she, and quite ill.

They had no medical insurance of any kind, so she had to care for him alone as well as work a job. All they had was her minimum wage income.

They lived out in the desert in a small trailer. He was in the early stages of Alzheimer's, and she was reluctant to leave him alone while working. She was so afraid he would wander into the desert and disappear. She asked me to marry them as she needed the legal authority of a wife to begin to unravel the legal issues they were facing with the government.

So I married them in their little trailer out in the desert. Lupe, Karen, and one other couple were in attendance. It was the most beautiful wedding I have ever attended. As I began to read the wedding vows, I discovered they were redundant. Beautiful, yes, but this couple had been lovingly living these vows for 26 years. Tears began streaming down my cheeks. I was so humbled. All they needed was to ask God to bless their relationship which they were doing at that moment. It was truly a holy moment.

Also in attendance was their cat "Spice" and a wild rabbit they had been feeding for six months. What an awesome privilege for me to be the one to join these two in holy matrimony.

GIRLS
WHO HAVE
ACCEPTED
CHRIST
BUT STILL WORK
IN
BROTHELS

CHILDREN

By Kay Christiane'

Little children...precious gifts from God! Our most
valuable resource...!

Innocent...

Honest...
Full of wonder...

And yet...

You are murdered before you are born... And
thrown away like garbage...

You, if you are allowed to be born...
Are beaten...
Burned...
Broken...

No one seems to mind... It just keeps happening...
No one stops it...

Little girls raped...over and over... Little boys
sodomized...over and over.

You are bought and sold…like animals…and
used… Used for human sacrifices
Used for prostitution

You are kidnapped…
Brainwashed…
Yelled at…
Slapped…
Lied to…

You truly are the victim…
Unable to defend yourself…
Or support yourself…
Totally reliant upon adults and their choices for
you…

Or…you are allowed to run the show…
You are not given the discipline you so
desperately need…
Little children….

OUR ULTIMATE SHAME!!!

"Can a woman forget her nursing child, and not have compassion on the son of her womb? Surely they may forget, Yet I will not forget you. See, I have inscribed you on the palms of My hands"

Isaiah 49:15, 16 (NKJ)

JANICE

As we were doing foot detoxes in one of the brothels, she kept walking back and forth by the room we were in and peeking in to see what we were doing. She was very curious. So we asked her if she would like to have a foot detox. She kept saying no. We had finished with the last girl when she again walked by. I caught her and told her we could just give her a foot rub if she would like. She finally agreed, came in, sat down, and we proceeded to soak her feet in hot water and wash her feet.

She explained she couldn't do the detox as the electric current might stimulate a seizure. As we visited with her, she continued sharing the reason she had seizures. She was married to a man who belonged to a very strong union in southern California. Her husband had a lot of power because of his union position. He liked physically abusing her. So he beat her so badly two or three times that she was hospitalized. She had gone to the authorities several times seeking some kind of protection, but they would not help her. The last time he beat her injured her brain, so that now she had seizures. She was afraid he would kill her if she stayed. So she left and came to Nevada to work in one of the brothels. She had a service dog that would warn her when she was going to have another seizure. The owner of the brothel didn't allow dogs, so she couldn't stay there.

She had met that "special man" and he had fallen in love with her. One of the brothels had come up for sale and this "special man" purchased this brothel for her, so she became an owner instead of a "working girl." She really wanted to do something different with the property. First she wanted to turn it into a bed and breakfast. The county commissioner's would not allow her to do that. Next she wanted to turn it into a hotel. She was trying to phase out the brothel part, but it seems like, "the powers that be" in that county would not allow her to do that. It seems like anything she would like to do that would phase out the brothel, they would not allow.

As for the "special man," she proudly displayed a beautiful diamond on her left ring finger. We asked her when the "big day" was. She said she wasn't sure. She was still struggling with seizures and had to go in periodically for more brain surgeries. This "special man" has stood by her solidly since the beginning of their relationship. Praise God for him.

GIGI

She was young, late 20's, beautiful long blond hair. Such a sweet spirit. We had seen her often when eating and praying. Always happy and smiling. She came to our first church service. After the praise and worship she asked to have Jesus come and live in her heart. So He did.

Her husband was her pimp. She wanted a baby and eventually she had two. We baptized her in water six months later. The girls tell us they see her occasionally, but not often. We do not know if she is still a "working girl" or not. Her dream was to work with children. Her parents and family were aware of her prostitution and supported her in this.

She especially loved the roses we used to bring, until they wouldn't let us bring them anymore. However, we would bring one once in a while for her. We know she is saved and baptized in water and even though her family and husband encourage her prostitution, the scriptures tell us, "He will never give up on her."

"Now Joshua the son of Nun sent out 2 men from Acacia Grove to spy secretly, saying, 'Go, view the land, especially Jericho.' So they went, and came to the house of a harlot named Rahab, and lodged there."

"Now the city shall be doomed by the Lord to destruction, it and all who are in it. Only Rahab the harlot shall live, she and all who are with her in the house, because she hid the messengers whom Joshua sent to spy out Jericho."

"And Joshua spared Rahab the harlot, her father's household, and all that she had. So she dwells in Israel to this day, because she hid the messengers whom Joshua sent to spy out Jericho."

Joshua 2:1, 6:17, 18(NKJ)

Rahab is in the lineage of Jesus Christ
Matt. 1:1-16 (NKJ)

HADASSAH

She flew into Las Vegas from New York, had a Jewish background but is definitely a Messianic Jew. She wanted me to pick her up at the airport and take her back when she had filled her contract. We always prayed for a large room for her as she would often have prayer and bible study in her room at the brothel. She was and is an amazing woman of God. She has been responsible for leading countless women to the Lord in the brothel.

If given the opportunity, she has even led her clients to the Lord. Often we would supply her with books, CD's or DVD's to give to anyone in the brothel who wanted them. Many times she would get clients who just wanted her companionship and there were times when the client could not perform. She would then spend that time talking to him about Jesus. This lady truly did bloom where she was planted.

THE GOLD CHAIN

By Kay Christiane'

I have found a very tiny delicate gold chain in the bottom of my jewelry box. It was tangled and so I decided to unravel it.

I worked, trying to straighten it out, carefully turning and gently pulling it apart to find a way to make it useable.

I had to undo the clasp so it could be free to be untangled, then pull it apart where there were tiny knots, and undo the knots.

It took time and patience. But the knots loosed and I was then able to re-thread the chain and undo the knots.

Is that what you are doing with me now, God? Is my life like the gold chain, tiny, delicate and maybe worth the time it takes to unravel it and work out the knots?

It seems so.

GIRLS WHOSE PRESENT LOCATION IS UNKNOWN

<u>REBECCA</u>

When we buzzed in to drop off the roses, the brothel hostess was not very friendly. Rebecca was standing behind the hostess and exclaimed, "Oh, these are the Jesus ladies that bring us gifts!" I said "yes" and she very boldly said, "I want to talk with you." She invited us to her room. We followed her, although the hostess obviously did not approve, but the girl insisted. When in her room, she motioned us to sit down on her bed and began asking a lot of questions about Jesus. She said she was a Mormon but wanted to know Jesus better. She loved Joyce Meyer, so we left her with teachings and books by Joyce.

The next week we came again and she again wanted to talk. So I went to her room again. She shared how when she was 14 years old and home alone, two Mormon missionaries knocked at the door. She answered the door. They came in and both of them raped her. When her mother came home and found her hurt, bloody and hysterical, she told her it was her fault, and that she was going to tell the church bishop, which she did. The two Mormon Missionaries were not disciplined at all. Her mother sent her to work in the brothels as soon as they would take her and demanded she send most of her earnings home.

So here is a mother who was pimping her daughter in the brothels. Rebecca lived most of her life in the brothels. The only home she ever had was with her mother, who made it clear to her she didn't want her there. She never married or had children. Her mother told her she needed to stay in the brothels and send money home to support the Mormon Church and educate her nieces and nephews.

Rebecca developed a serious illness and was sick a lot. The last I heard from her, I believe she was on the streets in Las Vegas and on drugs and alcohol. I doubt she is still alive. She is one that called me Mom and she truly broke my heart.

PRETTY BABY

We were out at the ranch to have our weekly dinner. It happened to be my birthday, so there was a cake, ice cream, hats, etc. All of our team members were there, so we filled up a booth. Many of the girls stopped by our booth to wish me a happy birthday. Of course we shared the cake and ice cream with everyone in the bar.

She was sitting at a high table, close to our booth, and kept glancing over at us. I got up and went over to her and asked if she would like a piece of cake. She declined, but thanked me. I knew she really wanted to come over and join us. I had seen her three or four times before, and I was sure she knew who we were. She looked so sad and lonely, my heart went out to her. It was as if she was glued to her chair. Anyone looking that sad should have been in tears. I guess I saw her silent tears.

As we got up to leave, she reached out for me. As I drew closer to her, she removed a beautiful rosary she was wearing under her dress and gave it to me and simply said, "Happy Birthday." I didn't want to accept it because I knew she was wearing it for protection, but she insisted. I still have the beautiful gift and I pray for her every time I look at it.

HANNAH

She was drawn to us like a magnet. She had a teaching credential from California, was a lovely girl, and wanted badly to go back to teaching. She felt she wouldn't be able to because of her current job as a prostitute.

Her boyfriend was her pimp. She was buying him an expensive house in California and supporting him. I'm sure he insisted she stay and make "big" money. She didn't take many breaks. She was "working" months at a time.

When we discovered her birth date we gave her a lovely party. She had not had a birthday party since she was four years old. She took several of T. D. Jakes' books. He was her hero.

We haven't seen her for a couple of years. We want to believe she got rid of her pimp and went back to teaching, but we don't know. We do know she is a believer in Jesus. We also know God will never give up on her.

CRYSTAL

She was there to make money. She needed money badly.

Her husband from El Salvador had stolen her two babies from her and moved them out of the country. This caused her heart to break. Now she was "working" to get money for an attorney to get her babies back.

I could see a hole in her heart from losing her babies. She was very nervous, intense and extremely focused. There was a strong sense of desperation about her.

She asked to be baptized in water, so we made it possible.

She remained at the brothel for six months or a year, but then she left.

We do pray she was able to recover her babies. We know that God is with her.

GIRLS

DELIVERED

AND

OUT

OF THE

BROTHELS

"And behold, a woman in the city who was a sinner, when she knew that Jesus sat at the table in the Pharisee's house, brought an alabaster flask of fragrant oil, and stood at this feet behind him weeping; and she began to wash his feet with her tears, and wiped them with the hair of her head; and she kissed his feet and anointed them with the fragrant oil. Now when the Pharisee who had invited him saw this, he spoke to himself, saying, 'This Man, if He were a prophet, would know who and what manner of woman this is who is touching Him, for she is a sinner."

Then He turned to the woman and said to Simon, 'Do you see this woman? I entered your house; you gave Me no water for My feet, but she had washed My feet with her tears and wiped them with the hair of her head. You gave Me no kiss, but this woman has not ceased to kiss My feet since the time I came in. You did not anoint My head with oil, but this woman has anointed My feet with fragrant oil. Therefore I say to you, her sins, which are many, are forgiven, for she loved much. But to whom little is forgiven, the same loves little.' Then He said to her, 'Your sins are forgiven.'"

Luke 7:37-39, 44-48 (NKJ)

STORMIE

This one always helped us spread out the gifts on a bed. After her foot detox, she would take the other girls and show them all the resources we had on display, all the while encouraging them to select this or that CD or book. She really loved us and we loved her.

As she was already a believer, we always gave her the newest books and CD's. She had issues with alcohol and drugs, but when she went home, she was involved in a good solid twelve-step program. Her boyfriend, who was also into drugs and alcohol, was not in a twelve-step program.

We kept her in prayer. Soon she seemed to be taking better care of herself. She had dental work done which she badly needed. Then she found a good job in her home town. She was able to work for a month there and then come out to the brothels for a month.

After a while, she started working her job at home for a longer period of time, and worked less time in the brothels. Then finally, she stayed home, quit the brothels and became clean and sober.

I still hear from her occasionally. She is still clean and sober, and has received several promotions on her job.

By the way, her boyfriend is now also attending a twelve-step program. Remember this "getting out" is a process, but God wins again. Yeah God!

GOD REALLY DOES HEAR AND ANSWER PRAYER!

JASMINE

This one was so special. Such a sweet spirit. She always looked forward to our monthly visits. She was always so concerned for her mother, as she had physical issues. She sent a lot of money to her mom and always asked us to pray for her mom. She had never married and had no children. She started taking a lot of Joyce Meyer books and CD's from us. One month when we were there, she again asked for prayer. We found a quiet corner and I asked her if she would like to ask Jesus into her heart. She did want that. So she did, and Jesus did, and the two of them really connected.

A couple of years passed. Every time we would see her we just felt closer to her. Then she met a "special man" and she told us she would soon be leaving. And, she did. We miss seeing her, but we are so grateful she is out and doing well. It is always so interesting to watch the process these girls go through after their salvation experience. It just becomes harder and harder for them to stay and eventually God wins. As they discover the love God has for them they become more and more able to trust Him and eventually He wins. Bravo God!

THE INTERVIEW

Bombs were blasting, destroying everything around her. Houses were being leveled as she watched. Often she and her sister would hide in the sewers underground. At least there the sirens were not so loud. Playing in the streets was messy as her little feet would be covered in blood from all the dead bodies lying around them. Her mother and sister were trying to survive in a war zone in the Middle East. She was five years old.

Her father had abandoned her mother and two daughters, relocating in America. He was supposed to arrange for his family to join him later. He had applied and they had been approved. But, when he arrived in America, he met a woman, whom he decided he wanted to marry. He did not tell his wife and children they had been approved to come, because now he didn't want them here. In fact, he did not contact them at all.

Things did not turn out as he had planned, for when his records revealed that he was already married to Jasmine's mother, a priest said he was not allowed to marry his new girlfriend. Meanwhile, Jasmine and her mother continued to wait for word from him that he had made arrangements for them to come to be with him.

After a year without hearing from him, her mother

contacted the authorities and discovered that she and the girls had had clearance for over a year. So Mom contacted Dad, and they were brought to the U.S. and out of the war zone.

They were a family again, but a very unhappy family. Jasmine's father was a party boy and not home much. Her mother spoke no English and neither did Jasmine or her sister. He obviously did not want the responsibility of a family. Her parents fought and argued constantly. They lived with the father for less than a year. His lifestyle was totally unacceptable.

One day, in his absence, her Mom packed up their belongings and left. She did not know how to drive, nor did she have a driver's license. But somehow she was able to drive from Georgia to South Carolina where she knew one person who managed a business. That person hired her to work there.

Jasmine's father hired an investigator to find his family, and deport them back to the Middle East and the war zone. The INS appeared one day to her mother at work, but they were intercepted by the friend, who told them that Jasmine's Mom was engaged to marry a coworker. She immediately married the coworker, whom she barely knew. The coworker was a loser, an alcoholic, who trashed the house often in a drunken rage. He threatened her constantly with deportation and was physically and verbally abusive. Her mother had to stay married for three years before she could divorce or she would be deported.

Meanwhile, he was sexually molesting Jasmine at nine years of age, while her Mom was at work. He wouldn't let her go swimming or play with other children unless she did sex acts with him first. This man was blond and blue eyed, which turned Jasmine off to white men.

Living in the deep south as a child, she experienced a lot of racism, was called sand n…. and treated much the same as black children. Often her sister, who was two years older than Jasmine, was physically abusing her as well. At eleven years of age, she was confused, hurt, and had seen and experienced so many things that a child should never have experienced. She was diagnosed with ADD and post traumatic syndrome.

Her little girl heart needed a father to love and protect her; to tell her she was beautiful and loved. That never happened, nor has it yet happened.

As soon as her mother's divorce was over, they moved to California where there were lots of dark people like her. She no longer was called sand n.... and no longer had to suffer the racism she had experienced.

We met her five years ago. She was so kind to us, always offering water and making us feel so welcome. She greatly appreciated the gifts we brought. When asked if she would want us to pray for anything specific, she always wanted prayer for her mother. After a year I asked if she would like a personal relationship with Jesus; she said "yes." We found a quiet corner in the brothel, and she received Jesus as her Lord and savior. Immediately she began listening to the CDs we brought, and Christian music and Christian stations on her computer. She could not get enough of her new-found Savior.

I remember one visit where Jasmine and another girl were being stalked by some demonic spirits. We had left the brothel and were in the van. The other girl came into the parking lot, looking for us. I went back in the brothel, found a quiet corner and prayed with them for protection. I left Joyce Meyer's book, THE NAME, THE WORD, AND THE BLOOD. I also gave them a Bible and showed them Psalms 91. Jasmine later told me she started reading Psalms 91 every day, and now she has it memorized. She also has put a Bible on her I-phone.

While in college in California, she met a good looking man. He owned a hair salon, had a nice car, a done up Lexus, nice house, swimming pool, pool room... impressive, huh? She started dating him. He bought her expensive jewelry. They started having sex on their fourth date. He told her how much he loved her, sent her flowers. All the things a good pimp does. Six months later he asked her to be his hooker.

She said, "What made me say, I'll be a hooker for you? It was the money!" Twenty-one years old, and look at what he was offering her. He promised she would only have to do this for one year. He sold her the dream.

At that time the legal brothels in Nevada would only take girls who had pimps. So instead of putting his girls on the streets, he put them into legal brothels. First trip to the brothel, he took her shopping, bought her "work clothes" and shoes, and had her nails and hair done. She wrote a note to her mother telling her she was OK, but was going to work someplace else. She left home at 21 years of age. It was her first trip and she was scared.

Old Bridge Ranch was owned and operated by Hells Angels. She started with a ten minute party, first doing quantity. She did cheaper parties, but more of them. As she learned, she charged more and had fewer parties. She had a germ phobia and said, "I didn't want to open up. I wanted to save something of myself, but all I could see was the money." The money was a high. It was fun. It was constant. The money was numbing you. You didn't have time to think about what you were doing.

She became excited about giving her pimp a large amount of money every week. She thought she was doing it for "us." She was always paid in cash and after every trick she got paid. She had a special place where she stashed her money in her room and, at the end of her shift, she would take it all out and worship it.

"As you get older, you get wiser." She was almost 25 years old, and finally caught on to what her pimp was doing…she had finally figured it out. "I'm paying for the

FANTASY, just as the trick is paying for a FANTASY. I'm paying for everything. I don't want to share a man. I bought an expensive lie."

She lived with her pimp in another state. For the first year she worked two weeks in the brothel, then home with pimp for four days. Second and third years, she worked two and a half weeks in the brothel, then home with pimp for five days. After that she worked three weeks at brothel and home ten days. She said she gave her pimp over one million dollars in six years. He kept up the lies, "It's just for us, there are no other girls, and you are the only one. However, he had only asked for one year and it had turned into six.

One day, while home with her pimp, she asked God if she should continue with him and, if so, to give her a sign of some kind. (This happened before she was saved.) Later, while rummaging around in a closet, she discovered a video. She played it, and lo and behold, it was a home sex video of her pimp, another guy and another girl, a sex threesome. They were obviously on drugs and this was an hour long performance. She had just asked God to show her a sign and suddenly this video appeared.

Immediately she left her pimp. He had groomed her

well. The damage had been done. He taught her she could only enjoy sex with him, so she couldn't enjoy sex with the tricks. The tricks were only for money, not pleasure. She would not allow kissing, nor vaginal petting, nor oral sex. She was totally shut down sexually. It was all show. At the end of a shift, she would smoke a joint. When dating men outside of prostitution she had trouble being intimate. She automatically started hustling her date, then was unable to enjoy sex with them once she charged them money. Her mind would not let her enjoy sex with anyone but her pimp.

Her pimp tried to get her back for eleven months. He tried to trick her into meeting him, but by the grace of God she refused to meet him in person. She told him she was with someone else, and changed her phone number.

When I interviewed her, I was able to meet her husband, whom she recently married. She has quit prostitution altogether. Jasmine shared a DVD of her wedding with me. What a beautiful bride she was. They live in a wonderful older home. She still has a special gift of hospitality. She invited me to stay overnight with them for a couple of nights and is still bringing me bottles of water. I was very impressed with her husband. What a kind and gentle man. They hope to have children soon.

Jasmine, how we love you. We pray that God will bless you soon with children.

COLORADO GIRL

One day as we were in a brothel eating and praying, we saw a new girl pacing back and forth, back and forth. Finally she came over to our table. We invited her to sit and visit. She sat down and asked who we were. We told her we were the Jesus ladies, and we bring books, CD's, gifts for the girls, always at no charge. She took some Joyce Meyer material.

She told us she was a Christian, but because of the economy, she had to go to work. Her husband was an architect, and was close to losing his business and their home. They had four children and badly needed money. She was looking on the internet and found this brothel. She applied and was accepted. She knew nothing about brothels and said she had been very nervous since her arrival. She asked us to pray for her, and of course we did.

The next week when we went back she said she had not made any money at all and just wanted to go home, which she did, the next day! That week I got a call from her, thanking us for being there and listening to her. She had quit and was home with her family. She said she felt God was protecting her while she was there, as she never did make any money. We were so grateful to get her call. She said she and her husband were trusting God for His provision. She profusely thanked us and encouraged us to continue visiting the brothels.

KIM

She was one of the most beautiful women I have ever seen. Long dark hair, very tiny and feminine. She was from Thailand. She used to come into my healing center for colonics and Megan massages. I saw her lying on the Megan bed for her treatment. She was asleep and so beautiful she nearly took my breath away. She looked like a porcelain doll.

As was the custom in Thailand, her parents had chosen her when she was a child to become a prostitute to support her family. She ended up here at one of the ranches. She was so proud to send most of her earnings home to support her parents and her family. Often she would talk about her native country. This woman had such a sweet spirit… so polite, gentle and soft.

For her birthday one year, we gave her a beautiful Thai Bible. She was so proud of her new Bible. Being the classy lady she is, eventually a very wealthy man visited the brothel, fell in love with her, took her away and married her. What a very fortunate man to have this beautiful "inside and out" little doll for himself… and she, I'm sure, is much happier now. Praise God.

RACHEL

They were to be married! So they went to the courthouse to purchase their marriage license. The clerk started asking her fiancé questions, such as his mother's maiden name, his father's birth date, and where they were born, so that he might fill out the document.

Rachel started perspiring and became very nervous. She knew she would be asked the same questions, and was afraid they wouldn't give them the marriage license because she didn't know the answers to the questions. You see, she had never seen her father, and she had lost track of her mother years ago.

Her first memory was of her mother taking a round Flicka razor, and pulling out her beautiful long hair at age seven. Her mother was very jealous of her little girl. Rachel had often been told that she resembled her father. Her mother hated her father, so anything she could do to disfigure Rachel's appearance, she would do.

When it was time for Rachel to get out of school, her mother would drive up, open the car door, and scream

at her to sit in the front seat. Then she would double up

her fists and hit Rachel in the face until she had a bloody nose. She broke her nose several times. If her mother did not come to pick her and her younger sister up, they knew she had probably gone off and disappeared. This meant that they would have to get home as best they could, and be on their own without food or lights for several days.

Her mother's boyfriends would come by the house when Mom was on one of her trips away from home and try to sexually molest Rachel. But she was always able to get away, running out the back door as fast as she could run, then down the rocky railroad tracks, barefooted, to spend the night at a friend's house.

One morning, her mother called Rachel out of the bathroom and scrutinized her face. Her lips were badly chapped and red. Her mother asked her if she had gotten into her lipstick. Rachel started to cry and told her no. She was grabbed by the hair and dragged to the kitchen sink, where her mother then wet her hands, dusted them with Comet cleanser, pried open Rachel's mouth and repeatedly shoved Comet cleanser down her throat.

The girls had a female dog who became pregnant. They were so excited and could hardly wait to see the puppies. But right after the puppies were born, their mother took a garbage bag, placed the newborn puppies in the bag, and filled the bag with water. The girls were forced to watch the entire procedure.

Often the mother would wake the girls up in the middle of the night, sometimes to scrub the floors, sometimes to watch TV with her. Rachel remembers one time when she was awakened to clean up a horrible mess that her mother and her new husband had made. Broken bottles of alcohol, broken glass and the stench of alcohol everywhere. The girls were up until four A.M. on a school night, cleaning up after the mess the couple had made while drunk and fighting.

Rachel's sister recalls hanging her jacket on a doorknob instead of in the closet, and Mom kicked her in the ribs. They both remembered being forced to eat soup with ants in it.

At thirteen or fourteen years old, Rachel started running away. She would sneak back in the house at night and leave again in the morning. Anything to avoid contact with her mother. She was desperate for love. She started playing with a Ouija board, and it told her that she would have six children. She was, quote, "looking for love in all the wrong places," and had become very promiscuous. Whenever she became pregnant, she would use abortions for birth control. Mother wasn't available, so she had friends drive her to abortion clinics. She had six abortions.

Rachel finally left home at eighteen, married an abusive man, and got pregnant with her son, whom she adored. The marriage lasted about three months. She then remarried another abusive man and had her daughter, whom she also adored.

When her daughter was about six months old and crawling, her husband began yelling and screaming at Rachel. The baby girl became so scared and upset that she crawled into the bathroom closet, trying to hide. Rachel found her and "drew a fine line in the sand." She divorced him and got custody of her children. She raised them by herself.

Rachel found a job in an athletic club. Soon she was promoted to manager and worked there for two years. She left her kids with a live in Nanny. As the manager of the club, she worked long hours so was unable to spend much time with her children. Her daughter was having nightmares that her mother was dead, since she saw Rachel so seldom.

Rachel then looked for another job that would allow her

to spend more time at home with her kids. She had met a girl who was making a lot of money at a night job so she could spend lots of time at home. So Rachel quit her job at the gym and started working at a strip club in Las Vegas. She continued working at the strip club for one year. She so wanted to give her kids a life that she never had.

Rachel was tired of sharing her hard earned money with the strip club. She had met a lady who had started escorting in a Las Vegas casino. So she quit the strip club and started escorting with this lady friend. She got involved with dominatrix because she didn't like men touching her. The pay was better, too. She had abundantly provided for her children. They were ready to be on their own, so they moved out.

She saw a lot of homeless people on the streets of Las Vegas and felt she wanted to help them in some way. The only way she could see to help them was to increase her income. So she moved from escorting to a legal brothel.

She had been working there for about a year when she noticed some very nice, caring and loving ladies who came fairly often into the brothel to eat. Out of curiosity, she started engaging in conversation with them.

"They seemed interested in me, and at some point, asked me when my birthday was. I told them, and they brought me a birthday cake with candles, a gift and birthday card.

"I was so surprised! I felt like someone actually cared about me for the first time in my life. No one had ever celebrated my birthday before.

"They also gave me Christian CDs, DVDs, books and other gifts. This was new to me, as I had never heard Christian music or Christian messages before."

"At about the same time, I met a working girl who became my friend. She asked me if I knew Jesus. I told her no. She asked if I would come to her room in a couple of hours to say a prayer with her. I said, yes, I would. I went to her room and she led me through the prayer of salvation. Immediately I was baptized in the Holy Spirit and received my prayer language."

"Soon after, I saw my friend again. She asked if I had ever seen the movie, 'The Passion of the Christ'. I hadn't. She insisted that I watch it with her. She was showing it in the lunchroom that evening at the brothel. She warned me that it would be very graphic and told me to keep my eyes open. As I watched the movie, my heart was torn. I had no idea that Jesus loves us so much.

After the movie, I went to my room. I had put crosses all over my room after listening to Joyce Meyer's teachings that the ladies had given me. I knew that I knew. I had to leave! I could not stay there anymore.

While lying on my bed, I saw Jesus in a vision. He was looking at me with hands pressed together, holding His head. With so much love directed at me, He told me I didn't have to stay there anymore.

The next day, I packed my stuff and left. I never went back.

On the fourth of July that year, I was water baptized. I lost my house, my car and all of my possessions.

However, I was always able to find a job, and I always had a place to stay and a car to drive."

JESUS LOVES PROSTITUTES

SAND CASTLES

By Kay Christiane'

I have made these plans like castles...
Cementing ideas and dreams together...
With the concrete of who I think I am...

Only to discover... I
am only a child...
I have been building sand castles on the beach.

When a wave of the Spirit comes...
The castle melts away...
Leaving the beach bare...

The child is left with just being...
A CHILD OF GOD

<u>LEA</u>

On the fourth of July, the girls wanted us to come out to their party, so we went out to the pool. We had purchased some sparklers and brought them with us. One of the girls who had been very shy with us, loved the sparklers. I kept lighting them and giving them to her. Soon she was laughing and giggling as she made huge circles in the air with the lit sparklers. Amazing what God can use to break down barriers.

From then on, she always greeted us when we came out, and soon would sit and talk, when not busy. This girl was a beautiful blond and always dressed very tastefully.

Eventually we offered her reading material, CD's and DVD's. She liked to read. We remember when one of her sons got married. She showed us the pictures of the lovely wedding.

Usually she would contract for a couple of months at a time and then go home. She disappeared for a couple of years. We discovered later she had been in an accident and had some major injuries that prevented her from working. Just recently we reconnected with her at one of the brothels. She was so happy to see us again and we loved being able to visit with her again.

We pray for these girls on a weekly basis. We also assign a girl to people who want to pray for them for 40 days. This ministry is based on prayer. Prayer is the backbone of this ministry. Without it we can do nothing. With it, God can do anything.

LEA'S INTERVIEW

Lea was born into a very stable Christian family. Her dad was a steel worker. Her mother was a bank teller. They had her when older than most couples back then. Dad was 40 and Mom 32 when she was born. She had a wonderful grandmother, cousins, aunts and uncles. Her father was Catholic and her mother was Methodist. She was baptized in the Methodist Church as an infant. Her mother instructed her in spiritual matters, teaching her nighttime prayers, such as "Now I lay me down to sleep" and she was always taken to church.

Lea went to kindergarten in a public school. She was

very shy and quiet but liked school. Her teacher reported to her parents that she was too quiet but seemed well adjusted. In elementary school she was bullied a lot, physically and emotionally, mostly by girls.

She lived in a small town and had a few close friends. In her town, only white people lived, Slavish, Polish, Italian and Jewish. Junior High brought the normal behavior, socialization began and along with it came an interest in boys, "girl talk," giggles, etc. No major drama however.

In high school she tried out for cheer leading, along with her close friends. All of her friends made the team except Lea. Everyone was required to do somersaults and she was unable to do a somersault so she failed. As a result her friends all abandoned her. So she told her parents she wanted to change schools.

She started her sophomore year in a nearby Catholic School. Lea was very happy there and met her high school sweetheart. She dated him for three years. Her father did not like her boyfriend and tried to break up her relationship which only backfired and she became pregnant. At 18 years of age she gave birth to a 10 pound baby boy. Her parents supported her financially and emotionally but they did not want her to marry the father of her child. Lea's father would not allow him to come onto his property or to see his grandson. Father won. There was no communication with Lea or the baby.

Lea enrolled in beauty school and she met her husband while going to school. Her son was two years old. This new man was charming, brought gifts and flowers and seemed to love her baby boy. Truly an answer to her prayers. He asked her to marry him within a month of their meeting. She accepted his proposal and in August of 1986 she was married.

Her new husband was in the Navy so she stayed with her parents while he was deployed. When he came home they moved to Virginia and she started housekeeping. Everything was great for the first 8 months, until she became pregnant and then he became physically and verbally abusive.

She remembers Valentine's Day. At 21 years old her husband wanted her to abort the baby. She talked to her mother about it and Lea decided she didn't want an abortion and refused to get one. The marriage got worse and the abuse got worse too.

She finally left and got her own place, and she went to college and graduated. Her divorce took four years and she was all the while supporting her two sons. Child support was very sporadic and usually was only available when forced.

After her divorce she moved to Reno, Nevada, where she started working in a legal brothel. Happy to put her pain and sadness away, hoping to start a new life, making lots of money.

Her youngest son came to live with her in Reno and got in with the wrong crowd. He became addicted to heroine and disappeared. She searched for and found him and put him in rehab. He had to go to rehab three different times. She paid for all expenses.

It was sometimes slow at the ranch in Reno, so she decided to move to a different ranch in southern Nevada. After the sad experience with her son's addiction and the expense she incurred, she kept working down south in southern Nevada, trying to save her money to build up her savings again.

Then HE appeared! A fabulous "high roller client." She

was able to save enough money to put a down payment on a house, something she always wanted. The desire of her heart! Her own home! However, this high roller insisted on seeing her outside of the house privately, which is against the rules in the brothels. Even so, she did.

When she was seeing him "outside," his personality seemed to change. He became clumsy, loud and demanding, very abusive sexually.

"He demanded every ounce of blood from my body... for his high rolling affair at the ranch."

They were out celebrating one evening and she had a very bad accident and injury which put her out of work for a year. The "high roller" became agitated because she could not perform for him. He became so angry he blackmailed her and finally got the brothel to fire her. She was forced to spend all of her savings on doctor bills and physical therapy.

Lea came back to the industry a year later to try to rebuild her savings once again. She says, "I'm still searching for true love and companionship."

She prays every day, thanking God for what she does

have, and asking Him for what she does not have. She said, passionately, "If I could relive my life, I would never, never, never, ever, enter this industry. By having had this accident God showed me that all of the money I have saved over the years was not worth selling my body to users and losers. Nothing is worth that."

However, she is thankful she can walk again. She said, "Nothing is more precious than a ladies' health and happiness. Money can't buy real love. It can only buy sex, which is very empty without love.

She is searching for other employment. Her mother and father are not well and she has not seen them for a couple of years. Her parents do not know what she does for a living. She has a granddaughter who she adores, but cannot visit, as she cannot afford the plane fare.

When asked what advice she would give to young new girls in 'the oldest profession,' she said, "It may seem glamorous at first but it's not for long. THERE IS NO GLAMOUR. Try acting, modeling, or better yet, use your brain. Go into sales, marketing, anything, but not this."

Her heart's desire is still to own her own home. She feels her life has been a TOTAL waste.

Lea is 49 years old.

Now What?

My precious daughter Lea, how I have loved you...through it all, I will never forsake you, I am always with you, I will never leave you. Always remember, it's never too late and it's not over until it's over. Come to me now and allow me to touch and heal your tender, bruised and broken heart. I am the mender of broken hearts.

NAOMI

Early in our ministry, we walked into a brothel, had lunch, and went up to the bar to pay. I heard this scream from behind us, "Jesus loves prostitutes." She jumped out of her seat, came up behind me and gave me a huge hug. That was how we met Naomi.

We bought T-shirts at Salvation Army and painted on the front, "Guess What?," and on the back we painted, "Jesus Loves Prostitutes". We had these T-shirts on. I guess wearing a T-**shirt** like that would get some attention, especially if wearing it in a brothel.

Oftentimes she would text or call me to pick her up or take her to the airport. She was always so happy to see me. Her husband was her pimp. **All** of her money was to be deposited in a checking account that she had no access to. She had to get money from him for supplies, pictures and clothes. She would contract for months at a time, seldom leaving the brothel. She had a car but her husband took it away from her.

Not surprisingly, she was into drugs and alcohol. I have no idea how she would have been able to survive without some kind of sedative. Her husband was not only emotionally abusive, but also physically and sexually abusive. When picking her up from the airport, I often observed the bruising of her arms and face.

She was a junior in college when she met and married him. Only one year left to finish her teaching degree. No children. Her husband did not want children.

They moved to California where she wanted to become an actress. Husband began having men over to their house to have sex with his wife and charging for it. He soon discovered the legal brothels here in Nevada and began sending her to them. She could make more money here and it was legal.

But when she would go home, he would still pimp her out over there. She only went home for a week or two every three months. He controlled her with his anger and sent her numerous texts and phone calls every day. He called her horrible names, constantly berating her. The verbal abuse was horrific.

Just recently we learned she finally dumped him, after

30 years of marriage to this monster. The last we heard she was living with her parents, is looking for work as a waitress, and is going back to school to finish her degree.

We have prayed for this woman for years. Sometimes it takes longer than others, but praise God she is finally free. She is a believer and looking for a Christian Church to attend.

RUTH

When we first began visiting the brothels, the hostess asked if we wanted to take a tour. We did. That's when we met Ruth who took us on the tour. She took us all around and would not accept a tip from us. She said we were like mothers. However, Roseann gave her a little card with a picture of a kitten on the front and a message saying, "God really loves you." She just kept looking at it and thanking Roseann.

She was the one who always invited us to come to special events, such as Fourth of July or Christmas Parties. This lady had the most beautiful legs I have ever seen on a woman. She was close to age 50 when we met her. She loved to sit and visit with us. If she was resting or sleeping when we came in, she made us promise that we would call her so she could come out and see us. She always said when she turned 50 she would quit and she did.

The girls were referring to us by then as "the Jesus ladies." We normally were not allowed to go to their rooms, but she got permission for us to go to her room. Before she would invite us to sit on her bed, she spread a clean sheet over it. We sat down and she got in the middle of the bed on her knees and we led her to the Lord. I will never forget this precious girl and the tears streaming down her face.

At some point in time she shared that when she was a child, a friend of the family, who lived down the street, invited her and her sister to visit him often. He would "play house" with them and give them money for playing house with him. Of course he would instruct them that it was a secret and they couldn't tell anyone. So she was taught from a very young age that it was profitable to have sex with men.

Her parents never found out what was going on with their two little girls. Her sister became an alcoholic, and Ruth spent most of her adult life as a prostitute. She put her three children through college as "a working girl." We hear she is retired from prostitution and happily married.

VIOLET

I was so drawn to her and her to me. Every time, for several months, when we would "buzz in," she would seek me out. She always took her flower and gifts to her room and then would come back to visit.

We arrived late that day. I was tired and not feeling very attractive to anyone. However, she came right over before we could even get the gifts inside and displayed on the tables for everyone.

"Please come to my room with me" she said. "I would like you to pray for me alone."

I wasn't about to pass up an opportunity to pray with her. So I followed Violet to her room, sat down on a chair, and asked her "what would you like me to pray for you."

She was very specific. She wanted her husband, who was back East and out of work to move out here and find a steady job. She then wanted to quit her job as a 'working girl' and have a child.

So we bowed our heads and I asked the Lord for exactly what Violet had requested – no more – no less. Except I thanked Him for hearing our prayer.

The next month when we visited her, Violet's husband had relocated and found a job. She was working behind the bar as a bartender – no longer a 'working girl'.

We were so happy for her. We were grateful God had answered so fast.

The next month when we visited her, she shared that she was pregnant.

We continued to see her every month.

She had a beautiful baby and eventually quit work.

Indeed God does answer prayer!!!

"Then the scribes and Pharisees brought to Him a woman caught in adultery. And when they had set her in the midst, they said to Him, 'Teacher, this woman was caught in adultery, in the very act. Now Moses, in the law, commanded us that such should be stoned. But what do You say?' This they said, testing Him, that they might have something of which to accuse Him. But Jesus stooped down and wrote on the ground with His finger, as though He did not hear. So when they continued asking Him, He raised Himself up and said to them, 'He who is without sin among you, let him throw a stone at her first.' And again he stooped down and wrote on the ground. Then those who heard it, being convicted by their conscience, went out one by one, beginning with the oldest even to the last. And Jesus was left alone, and the woman standing in the midst. When Jesus had raised Himself up and saw no one but the woman, He said to her, 'Woman, where are those accusers of yours? Has no one condemned you?' She said, 'No one, Lord.' And Jesus said to her, 'Neither do I condemn you; go and sin no more'"

JOHN 8:3-11(NKJ)

CASSY'S PRAISE REPORT

Her name was Cassy. She was a prostitute for 30 years – since she was 16. Approximately 1989, she was diagnosed with HIV. Her continual use of medications from 1989 through 1995 reversed progression of the disease, not ever to be active again as long as she is on the meds.

However, after being released from 3 consecutive, 90-day incarcerations, she stopped taking her meds for three years. When she was arrested again in 1998, she got clean and restarted taking her medications while she was in prison for 2-1/2 years. She has been clean ever since.

Currently, she is on Interferon treatments for her Hepatitis C virus which is a result of her activity of illegal use of drugs and alcohol. Her treatment began January, 2011. Since that time, we have been praying for her and asking God for healing, minimal sickness due to reactions of the medications, and overall trust and faithfulness in HIS Word. We have given her CD's and books to help her redefine her strength in the Lord, her God.

It was through an intervention by a woman who had a jail ministry that actually brought Cassy to be saved. It took many trials and tribulations to bring Cassy through one of her toughest times, which is, leaving prostitution, drugs, and alcohol.

For the last seven years, Cassy has been married to a

wonderful Christian man who loves her unconditionally and supports her wholeheartedly.

One of our team members goes with her to her doctor appointments, calls her, and reassures her that we are here to help and support her. We are happy to report that her last laboratory result read a dramatic drop in the HIV marker from 3 billion to 43 and 6.559 to 1.63!!! Her doctor called her to say she is in remission for now, but wants her to continue with the meds through July, 2011. We continue to thank Jesus every day for her healing.

(This praise report was written March 04, 2011)

FOR GOD

DID NOT SEND

HIS SON

INTO THE WORLD

TO CONDEMN THE

WORLD BUT THAT THE

WORLD THROUGH HIM

MIGHT BE SAVED

JOHN 3:17

(NKJ)

If you would like to know this Jesus that I have mentioned in this book, this wonderful Son of God, the God of Abraham, Isaac, and Jacob, cry out to him.

We are talking about the God who created you! And oh how He loves his creation.

He is waiting to hear from you. He will recognize your cry. Present yourself to Him and ask him into your heart.

To order more copies of

JESUS LOVES PROSTITUTES

For friends and family

please go to

www.jesuslovesprostitutesthebook.com

or

Send donations to:

House of the Rising Sun

PO Box 4012

Pahrump, NV 89041-4012

Made in the USA
Columbia, SC
14 November 2018